The Last Hope

T0316529

Ekpe Inyang

Langaa Research & Publishing CIG
Mankon, Bamenda

Publisher:

Langaa RPCIG
Langaa Research & Publishing Common Initiative Group
P.O. Box 902 Mankon
Bamenda
North West Region
Cameroon
Langaagrp@gmail.com
www.langaa-rpcig.net

Distributed in and outside N. America by African Books Collective
orders@africanbookscollective.com
www.africanbookcollective.com

ISBN: 9956-717-42-8

© Ekpe Inyang 2011

DISCLAIMER
All views expressed in this publication are those of the author and do not necessarily reflect the views of Langaa RPCIG.

Note

This play was written as part of a three-month consultancy offered by GTZ in 2003 for the evaluation of the Korup Project with the aim of highlighting and sharing some lessons learnt from the creation of the Korup National Park, through a period of full activity, to that year when activities were considerably reduced. It is a fine blend of the results of the evaluation and some carefully developed fictional, artistic materials for the achievement of an overall dramatic effect.

The names of the village characters are either identifiable pseudonyms or names that typically represent one of three types of village communities of the Korup National Park Area—park villages (those inside the park), peripheral zone villages (those that share boundaries with the park or are close to those that bound the park), and support zone villages (those far from the park boundaries but which also receive support from the Korup Project).

Foreword

The Last Hope offers a fascinating depiction of conservation efforts by protected area managers and the attendant conflicts with the local communities due mostly to the difficulty in balancing conservation objectives with the ever-increasing community livelihood and development needs.

Although the author has given the piece an artistic touch, to achieve dramatic effects, the play succinctly relates the story of Cameroon's first rainforest national park, Korup.

The Korup National Park was created in 1986 and a project, sponsored by the World Wide Fund for Nature [WWF] UK, was established in 1988. This project gradually but steadily grew in size, which marked the appearance of several other actors on the conservation scene: WCI, ODA, GTZ, EU, and WWF-CCPO.

Although a multi-donor project with shortcomings, GTZ maintained its role in promoting the conservation of the Korup National Park. In order to achieve a long-term sustainable conservation and development impact, GTZ and EU, in partnership with the Government of Cameroon and local NGOs, promoted various community conservation activities, including community-based natural resource management, community forest development, timber concession management, land use planning and rural livelihood improvement.

Experiences in Korup have been so enriching that we consider it a duty to share these with other conservation and development initiatives in Cameroon and elsewhere, which is the objective of the drama project.

I would like to seize this opportunity to thank the Korup Project staff, village communities, Donor agencies, Government institutions and other partners for their role in the implementation of the Korup Project and their contribution towards the realisation of this play.

Vincent Ndangang, 2003
Conservation Development Adviser, Korup Project
Technical Adviser, GTZ

Characters in the Play

ERA, *Secretary General of Korup Development Association*

EKO, *his elder brother*

KONDO
KOKO } *their cousins*
REKA

CHIEF KITOK, *village head of* Korup

HON. BEKO, *MP of Korup area constituency*

ASU, *Secretary of Eyuma Development Association*

MOTIA, *his friend*

MOKABOI, *Motia's wife*

CHIEF EFABA, *village head of Eyuma*

PROJECT MANAGER
EDUCATION OFFICER } *of Korup Project*
COMMUNITY CONSER-
VATION OFFICER

HEAD PARK GUARD
PARK GUARD I } *of Korup National Park*
PARK GUARD II
CONSERVATOR

TIMBER MANAGER, *manager of a timber company*

TWO YOUNG MEN, *his porters*

CHIEF OF POST *of the Ministry of Environment and Forestry*

MINISTER, *national level meeting chair*

EU DONOR
GTZ DONOR } *sponsors of Korup Project*

YOUNG LADY, *an attendant in meeting*

RIOTERS *against the Korup Project and Timber Manager*

ALL, *other members of a group*

DANCERS, *musical group supported by the Korup Project*

The Last Hope is the product of a consultancy sponsored by the GTZ component of the Korup Project. The premiere performance of the play, which was also produced as a film, consists of the following cast:

KONDO
PROJECT MANAGER } Christian Nwogbe
CHIEF EFABA

ERA
COMMUNITY CONSERVATION OFFICER } Philip Etim
MINISTER

EDUCATION OFFICER } Elonge Vico
EKO

HON BEKO, Orume Nelson

REKA
TIMBER MANAGER } Osong Lucas
CHIEF OF POST

CONSERVATOR ⎫
MOTIA ⎭ Nsange Samuel

ASU ⎫
EU DONOR ⎭ Moleke Ramish

MOKABOI ⎫
GTZ DONOR ⎭ Orume Chantal

KOKO, Paolo de Plaisir

CHIEF KITOK, Akime Ambrose
HEAD PARK GUARD, Aloysius Eni

PARK GUARD I, Armstrong Moromo
PARK GUAD II, Bokuba Eric

YOUNG MEN, Ekoso Sussan & Philip Esapa

YOUNG LADY, Orume Joan

Act One [1986-1993]

News about the creation of the Korup National Park has just been received by the local communities. These communities are not happy about this because it involves the relocation of six of them.

Conservation education is employed as a means of winning community support to the conservation initiative, but things still prove very difficult particularly because the new arrangement precludes the local communities from continued access to the resources found in the National Park, a forest that has since been their main source of livelihood.

There is bitter conflict with the Park Guards, which points to the difficulty in balancing conservation objectives with the livelihood and development needs of the local communities. The facilitating role of the project in resolving such conflicts and the need for intensification of education to redress the situation are highlighted.

Act One

Scene One [1986]

Korup. A footpath in the farmland of one of the quarters. ERA and KONDO meet from opposite directions.

KONDO: Where are you going?

ERA: Is that a new form of greetings? OK, you, too, where are you going? You find me already in your territory and all you can ask is *[Mimicking nasally.]*, "Where are you going?" Is it a taboo for a cousin to pay his cousin a visit?

KONDO: I'm asking because I'm coming for that my thing. You know it has stayed for so long, and times are getting really tough on me.

ERA: Kondo, what thing again? Every time we meet you bring demands of this thing or that thing. *[Scratches his head in recollection.]* I know. But is that what you can visit me for? Me, I pay you visits—you and Eko—but you seldom visit me. Is it because, as you feel, I don't have enough food to prepare you some- thing nice? Anyway do you know if I've brought it with me? *[Searching the trousers pockets.]* I seem to have left those stupid notes. *[...]* But why must you embarrass me like this? Eh? Besides in our tradition, is it not said that you don't ask for your debt in the bush? Wait until we reach your house. What I have brought with me is more important.

KONDO: What can be more important than my money, Era? What on earth can be more important?

3

ERA: Leave that thing! Take me to your house. *[They start walking in the direction KONDO came.]* Even if it were a million that I owe you… *[…]*. Is it up to the cost of the radio cassette that my son has just bought?

KONDO *[Stops abruptly and taps ERA on the shoulder.]*: Your son? Radio cassette?

ERA: Yes. Twelve-battery radio cassette. *[With emphasis.]* Twelve-battery. Not the four battery toys that people carry about here, disturbing my ears every day and night.

They continue walking.

KONDO *[Clicks his tongue in surprise.]*: Twelve battery! Where did he get the…? Why could he not help you pay your debts? I hear you owe so many people nowadays. Possibly because of the recent court cases. Borrowing money left and right. Ask your son to help you pay your debts.

ERA: Do what? Do I need my son to pay my debts for me? How do you see me? That is why I've always said you need your eyes examined. In fact, we should arrange for a check-up before you lose your sight completely.

KONDO: Did I hear you say check-up?

ERA: This is not meant to be an insult, Kondo. We all can contribute some money to help you go to Acha Tugi. *[Kondo gives a derisive smile.]* Well…But am I not still strong enough to…? I mean, what is all this? Have I not told you that I have brought you something far more precious than the twenty thousand francs for which you're ranting like a…like a... whatever it is called?

KONDO: Where have you carried it? Eh? Where is the bag? Or is it that small thing you are carrying?

ERA: You may even call it a purser. [*A short pause. Pointing to his head.*] Look, everything is in here. It contains more than what millions upon millions of those large Ghana Must Go bags can contain.

KONDO: My brother, I don't think I understand you. I fear you must have joined that bad gang of rascals.

ERA: I'm getting tired of correcting you on this. They say cousin, not brother. That is why I often remind you of what you are missing. I know it's too late for you now. No, not really. They say no one is too old for education. In fact, if we were in some advanced country I would advise you to start attending one of those Literacy Centres.

KONDO: Literacy what?

ERA: I know if they put you there for one full century you will come out dry like a dry stick that is submerged in water after it is smeared with too much grease. Never mind, your children can do it for you. I have advised you to send some...Those ones that are already big...Send them to live with me. So that they can start going to school before they get spoilt.

KONDO: Do you want my children to die of hunger?

ERA: Have my own children died of hunger? You people

often think that there is no food in my quarter. How many people have you heard fainted there? I mean. Come on! Look, Kondo, the children need more than just stay in the house and eat from morning to night. If I were like one of you I would not be able to listen to my son's radio cassette and pick up the news that I now bring to you.

KONDO: News? Is that all you have brought?

ERA: Look, Cousin, the news I have brought you can....Well, I don't even need to tell you this. Because you won't understand. *[A short pause.]* Please, let us sit down *[Pointing to a log of wood.]* there and discuss. What I carry is really heavy.

KONDO: Heavy! *[Observes him.]* What are you talking about? Is it true that you have joined that gang and started smoking that strong Indian hemp?

ERA *[As they are sitting down.]*: I reserve my comments, Kondo. I can't blame you for the absolute ignorance. *[A long pause.]* Well, Cousin, I can now find some truth in the dream you told me a few years ago.

KONDO: What dream?

ERA: The dream Chief Kitok had about our forest? I know I gave a bitter response to your interpretation of it. And you were not very happy with me.

KONDO *[Angrily.]*: Yes. You described me as half-blind? And you have since then continued to regard me as such.

ERA: And what is wrong with me speaking the truth? Do you see well? Can you see the lines on this my palm, what letters they form? Cousin, I think it simply means I'm concerned about your situation.

KONDO: You keep on insulting me. Remember you even said I still believed in things that our great grand parents abandoned many, many years ago.

ERA: Centuries even. [Surveying KOKO from his old loincloth to his bare feet.] And is it not true? I know you people don't like to hear the truth.

KONDO [Stands up abruptly.]: Will you shut up! I won't continue to stomach all this.

ERA [Stands up.]: So what do you want to do now? Fight?

KONDO: That is what you are looking for. And I can give it to you now.

ERA: No one doubts your propensity to start a fight. The leopard of Korup! Is that not what we should start calling you? But, Cousin, if the thing is so plentiful in your house that you now want to start giving some to Ekwe Society for fighting in the bush, keep it for me. I need it.

KONDO: Is that why you cannot pay your debts?

ERA: I am not poor, Kondo, if that is where you're coming from. I invest in my children's education.

KONDO: Education my leg! Is your son not back in the

village scrambling for bush mango with the women like any other young man?

ERA: What is wrong with that? Has he not been able to buy a...?

KONDO: Brother, you have spoilt the child. Now I hear he has refused to even assist you carry the bag while you carry the gun and do the hunting.

ERA: Let him stay. No problem. Let people laugh at him now because he bends down with the women and opens his anus to the sky to pick bush mango. But one day they'll be surprised to hear that he has been given a big office in Yaounde.

KONDO: [*Laughs derisively.*]: You are day-dreaming, Era. You are, indeed, dreaming.

ERA: I don't blame you. Illiteracy is a very bad disease. [*A short pause.*] Look, my son has good qualifications, if you don't know.

Enter EKO.

EKO: What is all the fuss about? Eh?

ERA: Is it not this…?

KONDO: This what?

EKO: Please, behave yourselves! Can you not…I mean…have you lost your sense of respect? See how you both could not even pause to say welcome to Senior.

8

ERA: Senior, welcome. *[Light-heartedly.]* But, you see, nowadays we need seniors who can actually defend their titles.

KONDO: Don't mind him. Welcome, brother.

ERA: Cousin, not brother.

EKO: What's the difference?

KONDO: Ask him. That is how he has been correcting me here.

EKO: Brother-o, cousin-o, it's the same thing.

KONDO: Yes. It's only you can correct him.

EKO: By the way, what has brought you both here? *[A short pause.]* Kondo, if my memory hasn't failed me, I don't think you own a farm in this part of the forest.

KONDO: No. I was on my way to his quarter to ask for....

ERA: Your debt. From me.

EKO: But you have to pay him, if you owe him.

ERA: I have not refused to pay him, Eko.

EKO: Are you here to pay him?

ERA: Yes and no, Eko. Actually, I forgot the...Because....

EKO: Because what?

KONDO: Because all that is in his head is to come here and insult me.

ERA: Was it an insult to inform you that my son has bought a radio cassette? You are simply jealous. Senior, Kondo is dying with jealousy. Because my son has bought a....

KONDO: Why should I be jealous? Why should I? What is a radio cassette?

ERA: See what I was saying? He does not even want to give me time to tell Senior the story about my son's brand new radio cassette so that we can arrange for him to come home and give the boy blessings in the proper traditional fashion.

KONDO: Must you use your son to insult people?

ERA: Is that not what I have said? Jealousy is eating up your heart!

EKO: Stop all this, both of you. You don't have to be quarrelling like this. *[Silence.]* Now, Era, what has actually brought you here? And don't you misinterpret me. Because you have every right to visit your cousin, too. *[Jocularly.]* And I know your visits are hardly without....

ERA: Eko, my mission here is to share with Kondo the

news I heard on the radio about our forest.

EKO: News? On the radio? About our forest?

ERA: In fact, I was even supposed to come to you first, but felt that since Kondo doesn't own a radio....

EKO: No problem. Just give me the news.

ERA: The news is that as we are standing here now, Government has taken the whole of our forest. In fact, the name has already been changed from Korup Forest Reserve to Korup National Park.

KONDO and EKO [*In unison.*]: National Park?

EKO: And what is that supposed to mean?

KONDO: It's only a change of name.

ERA: Who told you that? So you thought it was such a simple matter, eh? Look, six villages found within   the forest area will have to move out. And this may affect us.

KONDO: Move to where? I hope that doesn't include me. Because I won't step an inch from here.

ERA: That is my position too. I don't see how they can move me from my beautiful, sandy village. To start with, my quarter is so big, and they will only need to hire big bulldozers to push us out. Me to leave my Small London?

EKO: Are our cousins, Koko and Reka, aware of the

news?

ERA: How can I tell, Eko? It depends on whether they ever listen to the radio.

EKO: Are you sure of the facts, Era? Are you very sure?

ERA: When have you started questioning the accuracy of my facts, Eko? I listened to the 3 O'clock news. Yesterday. *[Emphatically.]* In English.

EKO: I know what you mean. And I can trust you. Of course, I've always done. *[Hailing.]* Sasse Boy!

ERA: *[Angrily.]*: Eko, you know I hate to be addressed by that name, don't you? As if I were not intelligent enough to attend Sasse College. *[Holds KONDO by the hand and starts to walk away.]* Eko doesn't seem to be taking this matter seriously. *[EKO starts following them.]* Chief Kitok needs to be informed about it. The flood that is coming is so wild and so violent that if we fool about it may sweep every one of us.

KONDO: I think we should plead with the women to dance round the village with their juju in order to soften the matter.

ERA *[Stops abruptly and taps KONDO on the shoulder.]*: You're right. That is definitely what we should do.

EKO: I support the idea too. *[ERA turns around and casts him an angry look, and then continues walking. EKO still follows.]* I don't see why I should be pushed out of my quarter,   leaving behind my vast land, my grandfather's grave...And *[A short pause.]* come to think of this. How do we transport our large wooden gong to the new settlement?

Sound of a traditional wooden gong from a distance. They exit in haste.

Gradual Fadeout

Act One

Scene Two [1988—1990]

In front of CHIEF KITOK's palace. Seated are CHIEF KITOK, ERA, KONDO, KOKO, REKA, and CONSERVATOR. A small sheet of paper in hand, EDUCATION OFFICER is standing as he presents a talk.

EDUCATION OFFICER: As I have mentioned earlier, Korup forest is more than sixty million years old. This partly explains why it contains so many species of plants and animals. And you can see that it is the last hope for many endangered and endemic species. *[In an elevated tone.]* On this note, I call on you all to join the Korup Project and the Government of Cameroon to protect the Korup National Park.

An applause as Education Officer now takes his seat.

ERA *[Looking about him.]*: Why did you clap? You people clap hands at anything that is said?

KONDO: If you were asked to stand up and say something, would you be able to say what would merit a handclap?

ERA: I bet you can clap at the pronouncement of your death sentence.

KONDO: Move me here! Book man! Have you not heard what a proper book man can do?

REKA: As if you read my mind. Our own book men here only know how to move about and make empty noise.

ERA [*Ignoring REKA, to EDUCATION OFFICER.*]: If I understood you, Officer, does it mean that we no longer have the right to carry out any activity in the National Park?

CONSERVATOR: That is what the law says. Anywhere in the national territory, that is the law. No hunting, no fishing, no farming, nothing of the sort. Only authorised scientific research and tourism. Even these other activities must be properly monitored and controlled.

KOKO: Why?

CONSERVATOR: Because everything in the National Park must remain intact.

KOKO: You mean we leave everything there, untouched?

CONSERVATOR: Yes.

KOKO: To remain there and waste, that's what you prefer?

CONSERVATOR: I don't think there is anything like wasting involved. Nature recycles itself and maintains its balance.

KOKO: Now that we don't have to harvest anything from there, do you mean that we must die?

CONSERVATOR: That's not what I've said.

CHIEF KITOK: I'm beginning to think that you're asking these people too many questions.

ERA: No, Chief. We need to get the point clear. *[To CONSERVATOR.]* I know as the conservator of the National Park, you are better placed to answer this. *[A short pause.]* Would you tell us what our benefits are, now that the Government has taken our forest?

CONSERVATOR: First and foremost, it must be abundantly clear that the National Park was created out of a Forest Reserve.

CHIEF KITOK: If you followed that track, and trekked and trekked and trekked... Some of you might take eight hours. As a young man, it took me just five hours. Just as you are entering the farmlands at Ikassa Last Bush. You might still see a sign board with the inscription of Korup Forest Reserve. The reserve was created in the days of D.O Edgerton. In 1937 or thereabouts. When none of you here present was born.

EDUCATION OFFICER: Exactly, Chief. You have such a good memory.

CHIEF KITOK: In those days I had to trek all the way to Kumba to submit my tax collections.

EDUCATION OFFICER: Thank you, Chief, for that delicious tonic of history. As Conservator has said, the Forest Reserve is what has now become the Korup National Park.

CHIEF KITOK: And what is the difference between a National Park and a Forest Reserve, Officer?

CONSERVATOR: That's a very good question, Chief. And the answer is very simple. A National Park enjoys a higher level of protection than a Forest Reserve. It is a very special forest, and the Korup National Park is an important asset not only to the Government but also to you all.

ERA: I don't understand how these two ideas fit together. On the one hand, you forbid us to hunt, fish or farm in the National Park. And, on the other hand, you consider it as an asset to us. How do we reconcile these? Or are you taking us for fools?

CHIEF KITOK: The idea of a National Park is still very strange to us. We have been so used to the Forest Reserve.

KONDO: Chief, you would recall when the project sent Reka and I to Waza Park. Did we not come back and gave you the story of what we saw there?

ERA: And is that what is happening here? If you look at the Master Plan, they promised to do this and that. What have they really done? How much support and how much development have we received from them?

KONDO: Rome was not built in a day, Era. The project has just started.

ERA: What? Was the National Park not created four years ago? With so many donors? WWF, ODA, WCI, GTZ.

EDUCATION OFFICER: Yes. In 1986 precisely. The National Park was created. But the project was established in 1988 by WWF. From then on the other donors came in. At various times. And who knows some other donors may also become interested.

ERA: So? *[A short pause.]* Are you telling us that all these so many donors cannot start doing what we can see...with our eyes?

EDUCATION OFFICER: It doesn't work like that, my own man. Concrete plans have to be established first.

ERA: But you have a Master Plan.

EDUCATION OFFICER: That is only an indicative plan.

ERA: Ehn! Only indicative, eh? Which plan then will you consider....

KONDO: Rome was not built in a day, I say. At Waza we were told that it took many, many years to develop the area. Let us give these people a chance, for God's sake. Let us give Officer some time to educate us. I enjoy the way he speaks. Just like orkat. Yes, like a white man from London.

REKA: Eh, Kondo? Me too I like the education a lot. It opens my head.

ERA: For what to enter? Water?
REKA: Hear that! Just hear what he can say.

KONDO: Forget about him, Reka. Now we know the limitation of their proclaimed knowledge.

REKA: I can't understand why you and Koko are so arrogant and adamant. Do you know you are bringing disgrace to us?

KONDO: Let them continue.

REKA: Our neighbours have changed their attitudes towards Government people. And you need to see what benefits they now receive from the Government. Roads. Schools. Health Centres. You can't get these by the use of force.

KONDO: My brother, they say development is an egg. It doesn't go near where people throw stones; it doesn't drop where people's hands are not together. So you see, with this our present behaviour, we will ever remain the loser. Because we want to show that we are so wise and so powerful. Chief, don't you think you need to do something about this?

CHIEF KITOK: I have always advised that when Government people come here we have to listen to them. You can never tell who brings you good news. In those our old, good days, behaviour like this would earn you a summons by D.O. Edgerton. He would invite you into his private office, order his men to lay you on the table and give you twelve on the buttocks.

KOKO: Those days are long, long past, Chief. Those were your old, bad days. Primitive days, I should say.

KONDO: But don't you think we ought to give them an ear, eh Koko the Great?

KOKO: These men, they are simply wasting their time, Kondo. No matter what they say, no matter what they do, my gun remains on my shoulder.

KONDO: It has been there for all these years. What changes has it brought in your life?

ERA: You can't see, that's all. And when I call you half-blind, you complain.

REKA: Koko, do you notice that the gun has instead made you grow older than your age? There is too much hard work involved. I'm soon throwing mine away.

ERA: And it will rust in the cold and moist of disuse.

REKA: Yes, let it rust. I prefer a casting net. With that I'm always sure of returning home with something to feed my family.

ERA: Black flies! My teacher once taught me that black flies cause river blindness. And each time Kondo goes out fishing, you need to see how they form a black pair of socks on his feet. Pick up the net, Reka. After all, you are clearly fit to join Kondo in that department of half-blindness.

KONDO: I won't say a word.

REKA: You can see only black flies, eh? What about the

tsetse flies, red flies, and mosquitoes that bite you during hunting? What about the ants and the snakes?

CHIEF KITOK: It's all right! All right! Have we come here to listen to you or to our Government people?

KOKO: Chief, tell Conservator that when next those khaki boys of his confront me I'll shoot.

CONSERVATOR [*Angrily.*]: You can't say that! You have no right to…

KOKO: Why shouldn't I? [*…*] What can you do to me? We own the forest. We are free to go there and take what we want. At anytime.

CONSERVATOR: Not any more.

KOKO: You have no right to disturb us. The day I meet those boys in that forest again, I'll show them what they've never seen before.

CONSERVATOR: You can't do that. Except you want to be arrested.

KOKO: By whom?

ERA: Why are you wasting your breath with this man? He doesn't even know that we hold the compass to the forest.

KOKO [*Laughs derisively.*]: None of you can arrest me, you hear?

CHIEF KITOK: Have you heard me say you should stop?

CONSERVATOR: Let him continue.

KOKO: It will never happen. Not even in your wildest imagination. If soldiers right from Yaounde could not arrest me when I *[Gives a meaningful cough and stops abruptly.]* Who are you, by the way? What do you think you are?

CONSERVATOR: What? Do you have a personal problem with me?

EDUCATION OFFICER: Pipe down, Conservator, cool your temper.

KOKO: I say who are you to think that you can arrest me? Who are you?

CONSERVATOR: I don't think you know what you are talking about.

CHIEF KITOK: Don't you know you are addressing all that rubbish to a big Government man? Do you know that he controls all the park guards? How powerful are you to claim that you are beyond arrest?

KONDO: Chief, it's only you can tell them that they're going beyond the limits. And if something happens, my hands and feet are not there.

CHIEF KITOK: Times have changed! In those our days

even a common messenger bearing a baton will pick you up like an ant. *[A pause.]* I'm indeed fast becoming tired of your unruly behaviour. Next time there is this type of meeting, I may be forced to leave you out, Koko.

REKA: Don't mind him, Chief. Some of us have loud mouths only here in the village. The moment we find ourselves in Mundemba we become as quiet as snails.

CONSERVATOR: Never mind. I can see that he is such a brave man. But no one is above the law.

KOKO: Here we apply jungle law. So warn those your boys. The other day they seized my meat. And auctioned it. Right in my presence, those thieves.

CONSERVATOR: They are not thieves. They are simply doing their job.

ERA: So it is their job to make us suffer, eh? They don't want us to hunt. They don't want us to fish.

KOKO: Because they want us to die.

EDUCATION OFFICER: No, my own people, a thousand times no.

ERA: How can we believe you?

EDUCATION OFFICER: I know it's hard to believe this. But, take note, the National Park is here for your own benefit. It is like a bank, and can yield you huge interests.

KONDO: A bank? Please, tell us more. How can we benefit from it? What type of interests are you talking about?

ERA: See him! See how his body shakes when he hears some thing that concerns money. In fact, if you bring out a bag of money and count it in front of him, someone can sneak in and pull out his wife who is sitting by his side. I must advise you, as a good cousin: Do not adore money like a god.

KOKO: Can't you sense that Officer is simply spinning out one of those familiar stories? Politics! And we are tired of politics.

KITOK: Stop! And let everybody listen. We are here to learn.

ERA: We don't eat stories, Chief. Let them bring us money.

CHIEF KITOK: Stop, I say. *[Silence.]* I must warn you. Very seriously. What? Have you lost your minds? *[A pause.]* If you see me stoop as I walk today, it is because I have carried the weight of time. And if you see me wear grey hair on my head, it is because I have seen seasons come and go.

ERA: I'm sorry, Chief.

CHIEF KITOK: That's all right. If only that is coming from your heart.

ERA: From the very bottom of my heart, Chief. Honestly.

Silence.

CHIEF KITOK: I had a dream. Long, long ago. Today I see that dream being revealed. We do not expect God to come down Himself to advise us. Officer, go ahead and teach us. Let those who have ears hear.

EDUCATION OFFICER: Thank you, Chief. Whether you believe it or not, the National Park is your bank. And everybody has a free account in that bank. It is a natural bank. You don't need to be told that Nature provides for every one of us. Free-of-charge. I must advise you very sincerely to join the project in protecting your God-given natural bank. If you allow thieves break into it, well, you know what you will have been losing. Use the interest as it grows but maintain and protect the capital.

ERA: This man is beginning to talk like an economist. *[Laughing.]* It's only a complement, Officer.

CHIEF KITOK: What's all this? When will you start behaving like people from other communities? It's a   shame! Shame! Even you, Era? What a shame!

Silence.

CONSERVATOR: We are here to see how we can reason and work together. For your own good. Well, you have all heard what your Education Officer has said. If you allow the animals and other resources to multiply, you will benefit in the future. Your children and your children's children, too, will benefit. Either by hunting some of the animals and harvesting other resources *[Emphatically.]*, in accordance with the law, or by benefiting through research and tourism.

EDUCATION OFFICER: Thank you very much, Conservator. And to add to that....Well, first of all, I'll like to know how many of you watched the play called Beware? One, two...Everybody, eh? Good. Now, guess what happened to one of the hunters. He became so poor and could not pay his debt because.? Have you forgotten the story already? Let me help you. Because the animals in their forest had been hunted out. [A short pause.] By whom?

KOKO: Foreign hunters.

EDUCATION OFFICER: Very correct.

KOKO: Officer, I really enjoyed that play.

EDUCATION OFFICER: That's right. I know everyone did enjoy it. Era, what about you? Did you enjoy the play?

ERA: Yes. I enjoyed the bit when the village-crier described one of the Government Officers as a man pregnant with beer.

KOKO: Was that all you enjoyed?
REKA: Once Era, always Era.

ERA: You, Reka, were you not almost sleeping throughout the play?

REKA: Me?
ERA: If you were not sleeping, put up your hand and

answer just one question.

KONDO: It doesn't mean that by keeping his hand down he could not answer a question.

REKA: It is even better not to put up your hand when the answer you have is rubbish.

ERA: You consider my answer rubbish?

REKA: You have just said so. [ERA jumps up.] What do you want to do?

CHIEF KITOK: Look here, you two. If you start that again…

ERA [Starts walking towards the door. To REKA.]: Be a man and meet me outside. I say be a man. Won't you prove that you are a man? Stand up if you are a man. Follow me. Follow me now. [He exits.]

KONDO: He was simply finding an excuse to walk out again. He is notorious for disappearing before the end of meetings.

KOKO [Laughing quizzically.]: I know his weakness. [In near whisper.] He simply can't stand hunger for a long time.

Uproarious laughter. Enter ERA., stealthily.

ERA: I heard everything you said. Everything. [A short pause.] Why don't you ask my wife to take a very hot iron and press my stomach to become as flat as that of a lizard so that there will be very little or no space left for me to store my food? [A short pause.] If your wife has condemned you with a fasting potion, look, let me tell you, mine has, since the day we wedded, been constantly trained to service my stomach on a very regular basis. And is it my fault that I am lucky to have a good wife? [He exits.]

EDUCATION OFFICER: That's all right. Let's get back to business. In Beware we also saw what happened to the Chief who refused to listen to advice. Who can remember why he died?

KONDO: It was because he transformed into an elephant and was shot by a hunter.

KOKO: No, Kondo, no! It was because Medicine-man could not find the tree whose bark would have cured him.

EDUCATION OFFICER: Exactly. Let's give him a big, big handclap [A huge applause.] So you can see that the forest holds the cure for the diseases that affect us daily. Already ninety medicinal plants have been discovered in the Korup National Park, thirty eight of which are new to science.

KOKO: Ninety medicinal plants?

CONSEVATOR: That is what we are talking about. The forest is rich, and it was on that basis that the Government decided to raise its status to National Park. [A short pause.] Have you heard about this new discovery in this forest?

KOKO: What discovery?

EDUCATION OFFICER: A vine that may provide a cure for AIDS.

KOKO, KONDO and REKA: AIDS?

CONSEVATOR: AIDS. Ancistrocladus Korupensis is the name. A very potent plant.

KOKO [*After a short pause.*]: Officer, did I hear this correctly? It seems like the plant bears the name of our village also.

EDUCATION OFFICER: Exactly. Korupensis is derived from Korup. So you can see that the name of your village has entered the scientific dictionary.

KOKO: This is not possible! Chief, this is great news. The name of our village has gone far and wide.

KONDO: It all sounds like a dream.

KOKO: Chief, is this not something worth celebrating?

CHIEF KITOK: I've told you our ancestors have blessed our land.

REKA: Our land is blessed.

KONDO: Korup is great.

KOKO [*As CHIEF KITOK stands up slowly in jubilation, opening his arms to the sky in silent prayer.*]: Long live Korup National Park. Long live Korup Project. [*More loudly*]. Long live Korup Project. *[A pause.]* Officers, we want you to keep coming to us. Regularly.

KOKO joins CHIEF KITOK in silent prayer. KONDO and REKA take various jubilant postures. As everyone else is variously occupied, CONSERVATOR and EDUCATION OFFICER engage in a quick handshake and snap their fingers and raise their thumbs up as a way of saying, "We have succeeded." The sound of music fills the air. A group of boys enter dancing merrily, one carrying a radio cassette on the shoulder.

Gradual Fadeout

Act One

Scene Three [1991—1993]

In a hunting camp. KOKO and ERA have just finished eating, and are set to return home. KOKO is tying the last of two large bags of bush meat while ERA is washing the plates, pots and spoons that they used.

KOKO: I'm happy with the way you've dried the meat this time, Era. You're really becoming an expert.

ERA: It's a matter of firewood, Koko. When it is dry, you have no problem. And wood is not so common around our hut these days. That's why I've always insisted that we fetch enough good wood and keep for the next trip.

KOKO: That's a sensible thing to do, Era.

A long pause.

ERA: Koko, have you noticed that we'll soon run out of pots?

KOKO: What?

ERA [*Holding up a leaking pot.*]: And this is the only one I thought was good enough. You know all these other ones we can only use after we seal the holes with grated cassava or cooked garri.

KOKO: Are you saying that it's only the one you stole from the Science Camp that is still good?

33

ERA: How can you describe it as stealing? I saw a pot in a strange hut in my forest and took it, and you say I stole it?

KOKO: Put me down, Era. I've not called you a thief. After all, if we cannot grab something like this, what else do you think we can benefit from those project people?

ERA: Is it even enough to compensate for the bush huts they have destroyed so far? *[A pause.]* Do you know that Reka now has a permanent hut?

KOKO: Permanent hut?

ERA: Yes. The roof is made of tarpaulin.

KOKO Where did he buy it?

ERA: Buy? Does he have money to buy a tarpaulin?

KOKO: So he got it from...?

ERA: You don't need to ask. The project is simply lucky that I've yet to stumble into real luck. *[Makes a discovery.]* Eh, eh! This pot is completely bad. Look. There is another big hole here.

KOKO: You over scrub the pots with sand each time you wash them.

ERA: Do you want us to cook in dirty pots? Me, I take my time. I make sure the pots are clean both inside and outside.

KOKO: You don't need to clean the outside. That's what is making the pots get bad so soon.

ERA: Koko, I have hygiene in my head. I don't hurry over this thing the way you do.

KOKO: Keep your hygiene in your house. You don't bring it with you to the forest. If we have no pots again, on what will you be practising that your hygiene?

ERA: I don't blame you. Perhaps you thought that the pots must live forever and ever.

KOKO: Amen.

ERA walks up to the barn and places the pots and plates and spoons on it to drain. KOKO arranges the bags on the floor and then picks up his gun and starts cleaning it. ERA sits down and watches KOKO, whistling a familiar song. Three PARK GUARDS stealthily walk near, and plant themselves behind a bush. The HEAD PARK GUARD gives non-verbal instructions to his team, apparently telling them to round up and close in on the hunters as soon as he blasts his whistle. Pandemonium breaks out as soon as the whistle is sounded. ERA and KOKO run for escape in different directions. ERA succeeds to escape but KOKO is intercepted and handcuffed by PARK GUARD II.

HEAD PARK GUARD: Why did you let him go?

PARK GUARD I: Sir, he hit me on the jaw with his elbow.

HEAD PARK GUARD: Shut up.

PARK GUARD I: Thank you, sir.

HEAD PARK GUARD: You are weak.

PARK GUARD I: Thank you, sir.

HEAD PARK GUARD: Follow him, and bring him back here. Immediately!

PARK GUARD I: Yes, sir. *[He exits in haste.]*

PARK GUARD II makes KOKO sit on the ground.

HEAD PARK GUARD: *[Turning to PARK GUARD II.]*: You are a brave boy.

PARK GUARD II: Thank you, sir.

HEAD PARK GUARD: From today on, you bear the title of BB.

PARK GUARD II: Thank you, sir.

HEAD PARK GUARD *[Gives KOKO a furious stare.]*: Have we not warned you enough? I hear they call you Koko the Great.

KOKO: I beg, sir.

HEAD PARK GUARD: You what?

KOKO: Please, sir.

HEAD PARK GUARD [Kicking him on the foot.]: Shut up. You are very stubborn. Can you count how many times we've forgiven you.

PARK GUARD II: Sir, I told you there was something going on wrong in our camp. [Picks up a pot and shows it to HEAD PARK GUARD.] Look at this.

HEAD PARK GUARD [To KOKO.]: What? You stole our pot?

KOKO: Not...Not...Not me, sir....

HEAD PARK GUARD: BB, pick up that gun before it disappears. And then join your colleague and bring that other idiot back here.

PARK GUARD II: Yes, sir.

PARK GUARD II picks up the gun and leans it on one of the poles that supports the roof. As he is about to leave, PARK GUARD I enters, panting.

HEAD PARK GUARD: What? Where is he?

PARK GUARD I: Sir...Sir...I met...met...with a group of men. They were...carrying...carrying...big loads on their heads. I think...I think...they are on their...their...way to...to...to the market, sir.

HEAD PARK GUARD: Did they see you?

PARK GUARD I: Yes, sir. And they started running

after me.

HEAD PARK GUARD: What! Why?

PARK GUARD I: I saw the other hunter with them, sir.

Sound of a traditional war song, so sudden and so close that its makes everyone tremble.

HEAD PARK GUARD: What? Come on guys, let's get set. Check to see that that shotgun is not loaded.

PARK GUARD II *[Quickly inspects the gun, looking up, right and left.]*: Sir,….

HEAD PARK GUARD blasts his whistle, and each PARK GUARD holds his gun on the ready. Enter a group of villagers, including KONDO and REKA, each carrying a cutlass or a big stick in the hand chanting the war song in a quicker tempo. They are led in by ERA who displays his prowess in traditional war as he brandishes his gun.

HEAD PARK GUARD *[As the warriors are getting so close, defiantly.]*: Will you stop, or I shoot!

KONDO *[Steps forward, arching out his chest.]*: Bury your bullet here. Right here. We are not afraid.

ERA: Our gods are alive. Ask yourself how I escaped from you, and how I stumbled into my people. Our gods are behind us.

HEAD PARK GUARD: Put down your weapons. Don't

you have the brain to note that I mean business?

ERA: The barking of a bulldog. That's all it is. Today we are ready to die or to kill.

HEAD PARK GUARD: Empty threats, gentleman. You are a joke, a big joke. And don't you let me lose my temper on you

KONDO: Do you think we are afraid?

REKA: We are already dead people. Should we be afraid of death again?

ERA: Release Koko immediately, or else....

ERA dances forward and rubs himself against the PARK GUARDS and everyone follows suit. Each PARK GUARD retreats, but with the gun still held out, as each demonstrator pushes him slightly.

HEAD PARK GUARD *[As he is pushed a second time by ERA.]*: I will shoot. I will command my boys to shoot if you touch me again.

ERA: We are not afraid of death. We want Koko released.

The traditional war song is now replaced by a chant of "Release Koko. We no go stop-o. Release Koko. Or we go die-o. Release Koko. We no go stop-o. Release Koko. Or we go kill-o. Release Koko".

HEAD PARK GUARD: Okay, boys, load your guns and wait for the command. This is fast getting out of hand.

The PARK GUARDS arm their guns. The villagers start retreating in fear. Enter HON BEKO, accompanied by a YOUNG MAN carrying small cage of bush meat.

HON BEKO: What is going on here? Eh, Officers? *[To ERA and REKA.]* Young men, what's happening here?

ERA and REKA: It's the Officers, Honourable.

ERA *[Pointing to KOKO.]*: Look there, Honourable.

HON BEKO: What has happened? Have you been stubborn?

KOKO: It's because I've been hunting, Honourable. To feed my family.

HON BEKO: Well, I know most of you hunt without permits. I've always advised you to obey the law. We in Parliament make these laws. And they must be respected. *[To OFFICERS.]* Officers, I'm Honourable Beko.

HEAD PARK GUARD briskly moves forward and gives a salute in the military fashion. The other two PARK GUARDS follow suit.

HEAD PARK GUARD: It's a pleasure to meet with you, Honourable.

HON BEKO: Thank you, young man. Are you the head of this team?

HEAD PARK GUARD: Yes, sir.

HON BEKO: Honourable. That's my title. Honourable Beko.

HEAD PARK GUARD: Sorry, Honourable.

HON BEKO [*Coughs.*]: I've been around for a couple of days now. Had a very nice meeting with your project manager. I find him an interesting and nice man. In fact, he even put a vehicle at my disposal to facilitate my movement around. I have just finished a contact tour of villages in my constituency. And I'm on my way back to my station. [*To YOUNG MAN.*]. Put down that meat, my good boy. You don't want to break your neck, do you? [*As the YOUNG MAN is putting down the load.*] It's small chop that my people presented to me, Officers. You know in Yaounde we eat only chicken, beef, pork and all that kind of stuff. Difficult to find any type of bush meat. Not to mention water beef [*PARK GUARDS cast quick glances at one another in utter disappointment.*] that I now have the privilege to enjoy with my family. [*A pause.*] Well, that's not so important now. It is the commotion that has brought me here. It started like a familiar war song. Then riotous sounds. In fact, the whole forest was vibrating. Vibrating! I could not imagine what was happening. That is why I've come. To find out what is wrong.

ERA: These people have been disturbing us, Honourable. Since the National Park was created. They don't give us any breathing space.

REKA: They don't want us to hunt or fish, Honourable.

KOKO: They want us to die, Honourable.

41

ERA: They have been arresting our people too frequently, Honourable.

HON BEKO: Because you break the law. You break the law, you face the law. And, let me tell you, no one is above the law. Not even me.

Silence.

HEAD PARK GUARD: Honourable, that man sitting down there has been warned several times. *[Pointing to ERA.]* Even that one was caught at least once, and was warned. But these people, they continue to hunt in the National Park.

HON BEKO: It is against the law. Completely and absolutely against the law to hunt in a National Park. The forest is vast. Eh? Eh? Very vast! Why do you choose to hunt in the National Park? Why? Eh, why?

ERA: But, Honourable, we are still inside the National Park.

HON BEKO: Shut up. *[A short pause.]* I don't want to hear that again. I don't want to hear it. Do you all hear me?

ERA, KOKO, KONDO, & REKA: Yes, Honourable.

Everyone hides their faces of disappointment.

ERA: But, Honourable….

HON BEKO *[Angrily.]*: Will you shut up! *[A short pause.]* This is what I was stressing in a meeting with your Traditional

Council this morning. Why do you think you have the right to cause trouble to a project that is here to assist the Government in important aspects of national development? I hear some of your so-called elite have decided to be a headache to the project. And I am forced to conclude that they are behind all these problems. What a shame! *[Silence.]* Officers, I can see you have a difficult task here. It's not easy to change the ways of people who have depended on hunting throughout their lives. You know, these people eat a lot of bush meat. That's what seems to keep them happy. *[Heaves a sigh.]* Well, I think I have no choice but to call off my trip. *[To PARK GUARDS.]* Because I find it absolutely necessary to take you to the village. So that we sit down together and discuss this issue with these people. I think what they lack is proper education.

HEAD PARK GUARD: Thank you so much, Honourable.

HON BEKO: It's my pleasure. *[To the villagers.]* Look here, I want all of you back in the village, eh? Straight to the Chief's quarter. That meeting is very crucial, and I won't listen to any excuses.

Everyone picks up their belongings and exits. KOKO is between HON BEKO and the PARK GUARDS who bring up the rear.

Gradual Fadeout

Act Two [1994—2000]

As a result of continuous National Park management and support zone activities, a new form of conflict emerges. This time the local communities are demonstrating against a timber company that has received a licence to exploit in their forest area, despite promise of development, which is eloquent testimony of their increased awareness and enhanced appreciation of the importance of conservation. From the discussions and arguments it is clear that the communities are becoming so prudent that they would like to consider the impact of logging before accepting its implementation.

A conservation constituency is being established, and the communities are beginning to take a proactive role in the management of their natural resources—natural resource management committees have been created in many communities.

Act Two

Scene One [1994—1997]

Late afternoon. CHIEF KITOK's palace. Present are CHIEF KITOK, CHIEF EFABA, MOTIA, ASU, ERA and EKO.

CHIEF KITOK: My long-time friend, Chief Efaba of Eyuma. Other representatives of Eyuma and Korup. You are all welcome to this very crucial meeting.

ALL: Thank you, Chief.

CHIEF KITOK: I will like all of you to stand up and introduce yourselves, one after another. Or do I need to introduce myself first? Is there anyone who does not know my name? Hands up, if you don't know my name. *[ASU and MOTIA put up their hands.]* What a shame! A popular Chief like me? The first Tax Collector in the whole region? A Chief whose name you can find in official records from the days of D.O. Edgerton? His Royal Highness Chief Kitok Ekaka IV of Korup? *[A thunderous applause. Smiling elatedly.]* Thank you. *[Applause.]* Thank you. *[...]* Thank you. Now, introduce yourselves. Beginning from my left.

MOTIA *[Stands up.]*: I am Motia, from Eyuma. Invitee.

Applause.

ASU: My father named me Asu Asu-Tam-Tam. But my friends call me Asu Boy. I am the Secretary General of Eyuma Development Association.

47

Applause.

EKO: My name is Eko. Quarter Head, Korup Traditional Council.

Applause.

ERA: Mr. Era is my name. Popularly known as Lawyer. Honourable Secretary General, Korup Development Association.

Applause.

CHIEF KITOK: Thank you all for the brief introduction. As I have mentioned, this meeting is very crucial. Last week my friend sent me a note about an important issue and we met and discussed briefly. And we felt that we should get your own views. Chief Efaba Ayukem, will you, please, throw some light on the issue.

CHIEF EFABA: Thank you, Chief Kitok Ekaka IV. *[A pause.]* My country people, it was one fine afternoon. Early last week. I was sitting on my veranda enjoying my son's children and their friends playing around. Suddenly, the children ran to me, frightened. Then I saw a long bearded man coming. He handed me this letter *[Removes a letter from his shirt pocket.]* Asu, take this. *[ASU walks up and collects the letter.]* The story is that there is a timber company that is interested in Eyuma and Korup Forests.

ERA: Timber Company?

EKO: Those people again?

MOTIA: What is wrong?

ASU: I can't understand why you guys should react in that manner. Don't you know how much development timber companies have brought to this country?

ERA: Do you mean the poor roads and the unfulfilled promises to local people? Or the negative impact of their activities that the local people endure after they leave? You can think of acute water shortages. Increased crop damage by elephants. What about...eh...eh...eh....All this happened in the second play that was performed to us some years ago.

ASU: You believe in a story presented in a play?

ERA: It's not an imaginary story, if that's what you mean. It also happened in some villages not far away. You doubt? My own man, you lack proper education!

ASU: Lack what? Do you know what you are saying? I am the Secretary General of my....

ERA: Stop bragging here. I am a Secretary General, too. And let me tell you, Secretary Generals fall in different categories.

ASU: What do you mean?

CHIEF KITOK: Gentlemen, we have come here to discuss, not to quarrel.

CHIEF EFABA: Asu, I would like you to read that letter for everyone to understand.

ASU: Chief, I don't think I'd like to read it. Let…let…let him take it and read.

CHIEF EFABA [*In an imperious tone.*]: I am asking you to read, Asu.

Silence. ASU stands up and opens the letter.

ASU [*Reading.*]: Dear Chief and people of Eyuma, I am pleased to inform you that my company has just received a licence from the Government to carry out exploitation in your forest, including that of your neighbouring Korup quarter that falls outside the Korup National Park.

EKO: A licence? From Government?

ERA: Unbelievable, Eko. How can the same Government that sent us a Conservation Project some years ago now include our forest for exploitation by a timber company? Are you sure that there is no error somewhere?

CHIEF KITOK: I am also surprised. But since this concerns the development of our area, well….

ASU sits down, still frowning.

CHIEF EFABA: I find it difficult to understand why you are still surprised, Chief Kitok. After our discussion, did we not agree on what to negotiate with the timber company? Did we not agree that our demands should include such developments as good bridges, schools, health centres….

CHIEF KITOK: It depends on how skilful we are in

50

handling those people. I find it difficult to trust them now.

ERA: True, Chief. If you recalled what happened in that play....

MOTIA: What play are you really talking about? What has a play got to do with this?

ASU: Motia, why don't you let them take whatever decision they like?

CHIEF EFABA: Asu, you can't afford to remain neutral on this issue. This is an important moment in the history of our land. Have we ever had this type of opportunity before?

ERA: Chief, those people are known to be very deceitful. They will tell you they are here for twenty years.

CHIEF EFABA: And they have indicated an interest in working with us for over twenty years, employing our children....

ERA: Ehnn! Same story as in that play. And when they come, they will bring you drinks of all sorts, invite you to dinners, give you rides. Just to distract your attention from what they are doing. And before you realise what is happening, they will have transported all their timber logs, packed all their machines and disappeared. Leaving behind a bunch of frustrated labourers who soon become poachers in our forest.

MOTIA: Are you suggesting that we remain in the bush forever?

Enter TIMBER MANAGER, accompanied by two young men, each carrying two crates of beer on the head and a bottle of whisky in the hand. The young men disappear as soon as they have put down their burdens.

CHIEF EFABA: Hello! Welcome. Are you the timber company Manager?

TIMBER MANAGER: Yes, Your Royal Highness, Chief Efaba?

CHIEF EFABA: You're right. Chief Efaba of Eyuma.

TIMBER MANAGER: I understand we are supposed to hold this meeting in *[Consults a piece of paper.]* Chief Kitok's palace?

CHIEF EFABA: That's right.

TIMBER MANAGER: My respect, your Royal Highness Chief Kitok.

CHIEF KITOK: Thank you, Manager. And you are very welcome. Please, sit down. Sit down.

ERA *[As TIMBER MANAGER is taking his seat.]*: So finally you are asking him to sit down with you, eh? That's right. That's right. I can see you are already deep into business with him.

CHIEF KITOK: Will you keep quiet, Era.

ERA: Ehn. It has come to the stage when you have to quiet me. To satisfy your customer, eh? A while ago, were you not against this whole idea? So you were only pretending, eh?

TIMBER MANAGER: What is the problem, young man?

ERA: You call who young man?

TIMBER MANAGER: Excuse me...Mr...What's your name Mr.?

ERA: Get away! What do you want to do with my name? Oho! Perhaps he wants to put it into his register so that I become one of his labourers.

TIMBER MANAGER: I'm here for dialogue, gentleman.

ERA: You can sit down for dialogue only with them. Don't you ever dream that you can put me in that your ring. [He stands up gradually. Looking sternly at CHIEF KITOK, in near whisper.] Let's see if there is anyone here who has the power to put all of us under his armpit. [A short pause.] I wish you a nice discussion, Mr. Timber Manager. [...] No. I won't allow you to put my own brother in that your ring.

ERA walks briskly to the door and looks back at EKO in surreptitious communication. EKO stands up immediately and follows him. The two exit.

CHIEF EFABA: Don't mind those young men, Manager.

MOTIA: They are anti-development.

ASU: I cannot imagine Era regarding me as lacking in education. Simply because we are holding a meeting in his village.

CHIEF EFABA: Hey, hey! Stop chewing your heart, Asu. We are here because we have something important   and common to discuss. We are here to discuss our long awaited development with our Timber Manager. *[To TIMBER MANAGER.]* Once again you are welcome, Manager.

TIMBER MANAGER: Thank you very much, Your Royal Highness. I'm, indeed glad to be with you today. This, to me, is an opportunity that everyone in this area must not miss. I don't need to tell you what I can do for you. You have read the letter, and you know how long we'll be working together and what kind of support you'll receive.

MOTIA: Sir, those guys who left a while ago could not even allow this my friend here to finish reading the letter.

TIMBER MANAGER: Never mind. Now I'm here in person. I'm here so that we can discuss together and plan for your development. I'm here because I'm concerned about the sufferings of people in this area. I'm here because I can and am willing to respond generously to your development needs. *[A huge applause.]* Thank you. *[...]* Thank you. Now.*[...]* Now. *[Silence.]* Thank you. Now, listen to this...*[As he is consulting his file…]*

CHIEF EFABA: Just hear that! I don't know why our people cannot understand.

MOTIA: See what those radicals would have prevented us from gaining?

ASU: It is over-know that is bubbling in their heads.

CHIEF EFABA: Chief Kitok, I think you need to shape up those your men. In my village nobody, I repeat, nobody can exhibit such rude behaviour in the presence of a Chief.

TIMBER MANAGER *[Coughs. Opens his file and starts reading.]*: We are going to exploit an area of....*[Stops abruptly as a chant of "No matter what timber must go. No matter what timber must go" is heard. To CHIEF EFABA.]* What is that, Chief?

CHIEF EFABA: You should ask Chief Kitok, Manager. I have no idea what's going on.

CHIEF KITOK: Manager, I have a bad group of young men here. It seems like they are demonstrating again. A few years ago they demonstrated against the Korup Park Guards. Right in the heart of the National Park. The men are really brave.

CHIEF EFABA: And you condone it? This is not possible.

TIMBER MANAGER *[To CHIEF KITOK, visibly terrified.]*: So what do they want to do, Chief? Are they demonstrating against me or what?

ASU: They are merely wasting their time, Manager. I guess they don't even know that you have a license.

MOTIA: Such is nothing but an experiment without protocol.

ASU: Indeed. A dangerous cause. A forbidden experiment.

The chant has grown louder and louder and is now deafening. Enter ERA and EKO, each holding a big, long stick in the hand. MOTIA and ASU sneak out through a side door. TIMBER MANAGER appears helpless between the two chiefs who are apparently very confused.

CHIEF KITOK: Calm down, my own people, calm down. Let us sit down and dialogue with our guest.

A chant of "We don't want him. We don't want him".

ERA: In fact, I'm so surprised that up until this moment you can't guess that he is not our guest. Is this not proof enough that he is not welcomed here? And you want to tell me that you do not also understand the meaning of the song?

The chant grows louder.

CHIEF EFABA [*In a loud voice.*]: You surprise me a lot, my country people, you surprise me. This act of open violence is a strange part of the tradition of this land. Where have you borrowed it?

The chanting fades into the background.

ERA: To whom are you addressing that? Don't you appreciate the intensity of what is happening? Look, either you send that your guest away now or he is dead.

KOKO shoots in, brandishing his machete wildly, which makes TIMBER MANAGER hide under the table.

EKO *[Hailing.]*: Koko the Great!

KOKO: This is him. The man who broke the thigh-bone of a tortoise like a biscuit.

ERA: Koko the Great!

KOKO: He's still alive and kicking. Where's that idiot?

ERA: Under there.

KOKO *[Laughs derisively.]*: So you've resorted to the baby game of Hide and Seek, eh? *[In near whisper.]* I didn't know that you're such a big coward. Come out here and feel the edge of my *[Brandishing his machete at him.]* akparanja.

TIMBER MANAGER *[Trembling.]*: Please, don't hurt me. Please.! What do you want? I can give you anything you want.

KOKO: We don't want anything from you.

ERA: We only want you and everything you've brought out of here. Out of our village. Today!

The chant of "We don't want him." grows louder and fades gradually as EKO and ERA start carrying the crates of beer and bottles of whisky and throwing them out of the palace, one at a time.

CHIEF KITOK: I don't think that is fair, what you are doing. In those our good, old days, in those days of D.O.

Edgerton....

KOKO: Bring Edgerton here and now, and we will cut his neck...like this.

CHIEF EFABA [*Shivering at the demonstration.*]: Ehhhh! This is a dream! [*As he is struggling to open the door to CHIEF KITOK's room.*] Chief, this is nothing to stand and watch. Let's help our visitor to safety.

KOKO: Don't you dare. Or else, something terrible will happen to you.

CHIEF EFABA escapes into the room, followed by CHIEF KITOK. ERA, EKO and KOKO pull TIMBER MANAGER from under the table and carry him shoulder-high. The chant of "No matter what. timber must go." intermingled with TIMBER MANAGER's shouts.

TIMBER MANAGER [*Offstage.*]: This is outrageous! I have promised to give you anything you want. Just let me go in one piece. What do you want to do to me?

Gradual Fadeout

Act Two

Scene Two [1998—2000]

MOTIA's house. A moderately set living room. Sitting on a table chair is MOKABOI, cracking egusi on the table. Enter MOTIA.

MOTIA *[As he is walking towards MOKABOI.]*: Mokaboi. *[Silence.]* Mokaboi. *[Silence still. In near whisper.]* Oho! It's a bad day today. *[Loudly.]* Big Mammy. *[MOKABOI gives a sweet smile and continues cracking her egusi.]*. I know you want to prepare my favourite egusi soup. But must that prevent you from standing up and embracing your daddy today?

MOKABOI: You left me alone in the house and stayed for so long, and now you want me to embrace you?

MOTIA: Come on, Big Mammy. You can't do that to your daddy. *[A little delay, then MOKABOI stands up heavily, embraces MOTIA and both kiss briefly.]* Ehnnn! Now you make my heart sweet. As usual. That's why I've found it difficult to leave this house.

MOKABOI: It's a lie! Since Monday, have you been steady in this house? And you leave me just like that!

MOTIA: I'm sorry, Big Mammy. Meetings. Preparatory meetings.

MOKABOI: What meetings for four days now?

MOTIA: Committee meetings, Big Mammy. Very important meetings. Did I tell you my committee members are coming to our house today?

MOKABOI: For what?

MOTIA [*Smiling.*]: To visit you.

MOKABOI looks at her stomach and then at MOTIA, apparently embarrassed.

MOKABOI: Why?

MOTIA: I'm only joking, Big Mammy.

MOKABOI: Oh, my God! See how you made my heart cut. [*She starts breathing hard.*]

MOTIA [*Feels her chest.*]: Ah, ah! You, too, Big Mammy! Why should you fear when I am by your side? [*MOKABOI gives a broad smile. A short pause.*] You see, Big Mammy, our big officers have asked representatives of all the committees from Korup to meet here today. This is the first meeting of its kind, and our committee has the responsibility to host it. You know what that means, don't you? That's why I've been so scarce these days.

MOKABOI: It's good that I've planned to go out and plait my hair.

MOTIA: No, Big Mammy. It doesn't mean that you have to leave the house.

MOKABOI: Look at my hair. Do you want me to appear like this before your guests?

MOTIA: No. I want you to appear nyanga-nyanga, Big Mammy. Even more than you've always been. [*MOKABOI gives another broad smile.*] That's my baby. The golden voice, the radiant smiles, the elegant gait, the resplendent look, the mesmerising shape—no lady can beat her in these. In fact, she's more than ever beautiful like a round, full moon.

MOKABOI [*Suddenly glances at a clock on the wall.*]: You've almost made me go late. You and your talk-talk. [*She rushes into a room and rushes out again. Walks towards the door and turns round.*] You made me forget to serve your food.

MOTIA: No problem, Big Mammy. I had some food in uncle's house not long ago.

MOKABOI: Are you sure?

MOTIA: Sure, Big Mammy. [*As MOKABOI beckons on him.*] What?

MOKABOI [*In near whisper.*]: I want you to give me another hug…for your baby!

MOTIA walks up to her briskly, and both hug and kiss. MOKABOI exits while MOTIA tidies up the room—doing some light sweeping of the floor with a broom and arranging the chairs. Enter ASU.

ASU [*Who has just planted himself on a chair, crossing his legs.*]: I met with Madam on the way. She's so heavy already.

MOTIA [*Struggling to arrange the table, without looking up.*]: Ehn.

ASU [*As MOTIA is still arranging the table.*]: That is not how to place it. You know, our officers have to sit facing us.

MOTIA [*Stands up, stretching his body.*]: You come and do it. Don't sit down there and dish out instructions.

ASU: Have you forgotten that I'm your secretary?

MOTIA: Is that why you cannot help?

ASU [*As he is standing up.*]: Just say you are tired.

ASU joins MOTIA in arranging the table, and in re-arranging the chairs. MOTIA gets into the room and brings out a tablecloth, and both of them spread it out on the table properly. Enter EKO and KONDO. Exchange of greetings—simple handshake or hugging—and then everyone finds their seats.

EKO: It's been such a long time since I visited Eyuma.

KONDO: Me too. My last visit was on the day you had that big conflict with the Park Guards.

EKO: A good number of years ago! Then it is obvious that I am more current on the village.

MOTIA: Massa! You people have created such a long record of war against the Korup Project. Eko, I heard your brother instigated that very problem.

EKO: Well, he had no choice but to save his cousin from imprisonment. But you may be surprised to hear that today Era is a champion supporter of the Korup Project. Didn't you see how much he fought to send away that Timber Manager? *[MOTIA and ASU smile quizzically.]* I know. I know you guys disappeared long before Koko the Great appeared.

ASU: Massa, leave man-o. It was all ignorance.

EKO: Ignorance is not good, my brother. Who could believe that some day we would sit down and discuss conservation with the Korup Project on the same table?

MOTIA: Have you not heard that the development of friendship after a conflict is set on a strong foundation of mutual understanding?

KONDO: Now you sound like my cousin, Era.

MOTIA: Actually I borrowed that from him. I admire the man; he is so intelligent.

KONDO: Intelligent? Did you hear that he spent a lot of money hiring a lawyer against the project? Is that what you call intelligence? Someone who thinks he can fight even with the Government, you consider him intelligent?

EKO: My brother is so difficult to change.

KONDO: Anyway, let's drop that stupid topic and consider something more productive. You know, my village is still very new to this idea of committee. We're soon going to be resettled. That's why we've been asked to start our own committee, and....

MOTIA: We hear you people already have farms in the

new site. Without a single house built. Isn't that crazy?

ASU: Our committee has already grown very powerful.

MOTIA: Very, very powerful, brothers. Asu, why don't you tell them what happened to a hunter who killed a drill last year?

Silence.

ASU: It was my step-brother. I don't know if you people know Chakara.

EKO & KONDO: Chakara?

EKO: Who else will someone know here?

ASU: Asu Asu-Tam-Tam, alias Asu Boy, of course. *[A short pause.]* There is no doubt that Chakara is popular. And he felt that since I'm the committee secretary and his brother he'll go scot-free. He refused to pay a small fine the Traditional Council asked him to pay. He thought he would still be the hero who killed a protected animal and walked away with it. But I, Asu Asu-Tam-Tam, I picked up my pen. You know me now?

ALL: Asu Boy!

ASU: The only one in the world.

MOTIA: Asu Boy!

ASU: The one with a sharp pen. *[A short pause.]* In fact, I picked up my pen and wrote a powerful petition to the Chief of Post, copying the Traditional Council and the Divisional Officer.

MOTIA: Asu Boy!

ASU: The only one in the whole universe. [A short pause.] You see, the first day past. Nothing happened. The second and third past. Nothing. Chakara was already moving about, bragging, hailing himself a hero. I had started losing hope that any action would be taken at all. In fact, I was already feeling humiliated, and I cursed the whole system. Why is it that action is often delayed in this country? I cried! But on the quiet evening of the fourth day, the Chief of Post appeared, accompanied by three gendarme officers.

Enter COMMUNITY CONSERVATION OFFICER and CHIEF OF POST. Everyone rises, exchanges greetings, and then sits after the visitors have taken their seats.

COMMUNITY CONSERVATION OFFICER [After a short while.]: We apologise for the late-coming. Looking around.], gentlemen. [...] What happened? Where are the women representatives?

CHIEF OF POST: That's exactly what I wanted to ask. You people know that the Government lays a lot of emphasis on the active participation of women in committee activities.

ASU: Sir, the women are very busy weeding their farms at this period.

CHIEF OF POST: That is no excuse. One day spent to

discuss and plan committee activities is not too much. If everyone were convinced that the committee was important then there would be no such excuses.

MOTIA & ASU *[In unison.]*: Very important, sir.

ASU: Sir, I should assure you that the Traditional Council and, indeed, the entire community now lend their full and relentless support to our committee.

EKO: Sir, without our committee we would not have been able to stop the use of gamalin to kill fish in Korup.

ASU: For your information, sir, elephant poaching has been cracked down by our committee.

CHIEF OF POST: I'm really glad to hear all this. And for your information also, we are soon going to have our first baby.

ASU and MOTIA look at each other in amazement.

ASU: Sir, how did you know that my friend's wife is pregnant?

CHIEF OF POST *[Amazed.]*: Your friend's wife? Pregnant?

ASU: Yes. Motia's wife.

MOTIA *[Smiling elatedly.]*: She's already very heavy, sir.

COMMUNITY CONSERVATION OFFICER: Congratulations! So you've been hiding it from me, eh?

MOTIA [*Smiling apologetically.*]: No, sir.

CHIEF OF POST: Congratulations, Mr. Motia. I didn't know that we are expecting another first baby. A flesh-and-blood baby. But the other baby I'm taking about is good news from Yaounde. [*Everyone but COMMUNITY CONERVATION OFFICER holds their breath in eager expectation.*] The dossiers of Eyuma Community Forest are already on the Minister's table, pending his signature of approval. And this may happen any day from now. [*ASU and MOTIA jump up in jubilation, hugging COMMUNITY CONSERVATION OFFICER, CHIEF OF POST and their counterparts, EKO and KONDO.*] And. [*More noise as EKO and KONDO also join in the jubilation. Over the jubilant noise that is now much reduced.*] And the dossiers of the remaining five committees, [*To EKO.*] including those of yours, are already at the level of the Provincial Delegation.

EKO: But, sir, there is one thing that has been troubling our minds all this while. We have learnt that all but the first committee have been registered as Common Initiative Groups. Why did you not register us all as NGOs? I mean why should only Eyuma be registered as NGO?

COMMUNITY CONSERVATION OFFICER: I thought I explained this in our last meeting? It doesn't really matter. These are mere nomenclatures, in my opinion. Because the committees will essentially be carrying out the same kinds of activity.

CHIEF OF POST: Exactly. And you can be sure that...*[Grumbling from EKO and KONDO.]* Gentlemen, don't you trust us? At least you can count on us on this. It is merely a slight, perhaps temporary, change in Government policy. And it doesn't really matter, you know.

COMMUNITY CONSERVATION OFFICER: Does it matter if you are called Motia or Asu or Eko? To me what really matters is whether the name changes you from what you are.

Silence as everyone stops to listen.

CHIEF OF POST: You can be sure that by the end of this year, we will have been able to push the dossiers to the next and final stage.

COMMUNITY CONSERVATION OFFICER: Let's give our Chief of Post a big handclap.

Everyone but KONDO claps.

KONDO *[To CHIEF OF POST.]*: Sir, why is the procedure so long? It does seem that my committee can only reach that stage in two or more years' time.

CHIEF OF POST: No. From every indication it is likely that the Minister might advise that the dossiers of committees in the Korup Project area be given top priority.

A thunderous applause.

COMMUNITY CONSERVATION OFFICER: You see, as I've always told you, the project is not sleeping. We keep on pushing, because we want you all to succeed. *[A sound of music filters in, and gradually grows in intensity. To CHIEF OF POST.]* I told you those guys might come. *[He stands up. Loudly as DANCERS are making their entrance.]* Surprise! Surprise! Surprise! Ladies and gentlemen, I have the honour to introduce to you Endemic Stars. *[A big applause. The music grows louder and then dies down gradually as he continues to speak.]*. Thank you… Thank you…Thank you, ladies and gentlemen. It may please you to learn that this group is one of the achievements of the Korup Project *[Loudly.]*, the conservation child of GTZ.

Another applause. The music grows louder and the DANCERS start to display. After a short while EKO, stands up abruptly, dances to DANCERS and slaps a bill on the face of one of them. KONDO, ASU, MOTIA, CHIEF OF POST and COMMUNITY CONSERVATION OFFICER follow suit. More and more people join in from outside.

Gradual Fadeout

Act Three [2001—2003]

Many community members appreciate the benefits they have so far received from the Korup Project. Unfortunately, there is a rumour that the project would be closing down soon, and this is generally received with a feeling of great disappointment. The communities feel that closing down the project would mean the collapse of the committees they have been struggling to build up.

However, there is a clarification of the situation, as flashback, in the project-donor meeting from which the rumour originated. This brings in some relief, as there is hope that some of the project activities would continue receiving financial support, either through the Government or local NGOs. It is disclosed that management plans have been prepared for the National park and two of the Forest Reserves, and that the Government would soon take over the Park Guards.

Act Three

Scene One [2001—2003]

In front of KONDO's house. KONDO is relaxing in a cushion chair, listening to some music from his radio cassette. Enter ASU and MOTIA.

MOTIA: Kondo! Kondo!

ASU: Enjoyment is going to kill the man these days.

KONDO smiles, welcomes them and exits into the house.

MOTIA: What did you expect? Look at his house. Look at every single house in the village.

ASU [*Clicking his tongue in awe.*]: Small London. Era used to call his quarter Small London. Today this is indisputably the Small London. No rival.

MOTIA: People who were living in thatched houses. Look at the type of houses they now have. Korup Project has done wonders! Would you believe that the old settlement had only two houses with zinc roof?

ASU: Lucky them! The people are really very lucky.

MOTIA: Look at the roof. There is no house around, except in Mundemba, with such a beautiful roof.

ASU: I say the people are really lucky! See what Era and Koko have missed?

Enter KONDO, carrying two table chairs. He sets the chairs and MOTIA and ASU take their seats. Then he slumps into his chair and turns off the radio cassette.

MOTIA *[Admiring KONDO's chairs.]*: Kondo, does every house here have this type of chairs?

KONDO: There are houses with better chairs, Motia. Life has changed. You need to visit our farms. The ones you saw on your way here are just small gardens. In fact, at the moment Mundemba market is too small for our supply of food. And we are already planning on inviting some customers from Kumba. Otherwise, our food will soon be rotting.

ASU: We really need to thank the Korup Project, gentlemen. Do you know that I, Asu Asu-Tam-Tam, alias Asu Boy, am now a proud owner of a large piggery today?

MOTIA: Asu Boy!

ASU: The only one in the whole wide world.

MOTIA *[Sneeringly.]*: So it means that I can have two big pigs from you in, say, two weeks' time?

ASU: Even if you need ten *[Stressing.]* now. I won't say come tomorrow.

MOTIA: Ten? *[A pause.]* Asu, how can I believe you?

ASU: Why not?

MOTIA: How can you tell me you can supply me with ten pigs today?

ASU: Ehn! I know. So you are one of those men who used the twelve bags of cement to instead make better floors for their houses, eh? *[MOTIA blushes.]* It's a shame that even you, of all persons...The project had a good plan for us, you know. But some of us took the whole thing for a big joke. In fact, if you visit my piggery today, you will weep like a baby.

KONDO: That is what I intend to do next. I want to keep pigs, chicken, goats and sheep.

MOTIA: All that for you alone?

ASU: Hear what he can ask! You have just started raising your family, mind you. And if you still think that you will continue to steal into the forest to hunt, and that that will be enough for you to feed your family, I want you to erase that from your mind right away. Right away! Because, as a warning, our committee will soon tighten its rules and regulations. And shall be very hard even on members who have continued to go contrary.

MOTIA: But I don't hunt protected animals.

ASU: When had you ever admitted that you still hunted but now?

MOTIA *[Stands up suddenly.]*: Wonders will never end! Asu Boy, were you not the one who woke our education officer up at midnight, after that very interesting meeting, and asked him to lock the door? Where were you going at that frightful time of the night? *[ASU blushes.]* Ehn! *[Sits down.]* Oho! You thought he would think that you were going out for...you know, eh? You thought he did not see the gun and bag you kept outside, eh?

ASU: That was long ago.

MOTIA: True. But, you see, you first broke the rules.

A long pause.

KONDO: My brother, one is getting older and weaker everyday. And a time will come when one will be unable to cast a net or carry a gun for a long distance.

ASU: Exactly, Kondo. Put your energy where in the future you will not strain to feed your family and yourself. *[A short pause.]* You see, the project helped me to build one pen, and now I have added two more.

KONDO: Gentlemen, I think I should fetch you something to drink. Beer! Because there is hardly any ofofo here. We've been taught it is not good for our health.

He exits into the house.

ASU *[On a serious note, to MOTIA.]*: You see? His life has changed. Tremendously. You Motia, what story have you to tell? What story? I'm saying all this as a good friend. *[ERA and KOKO, who have just arrived, hide against a side wall to eavesdrop.]* Imagine that the project built us a school, a community hall and, more importantly, a road. Was a road not our farfetched cry? But now that we have it, how are we really making use of it? Eh? Only a few of us have large farms. Only very few of us still maintain our piggeries. Only a few of us....

Enter ERA and KOKO, each carrying a bag on the head.

ERA *[To ASU.]*: Are you not supposed to be ashamed? Are you not ashamed that you stole the benefits meant for us from the project? And you have the guts to sit down here and boast!

ASU: Is it my fault that...?

KOKO: Is it your fault that what? Do you have a small patch of forest in the National Park that you think you merited all what you've enumerated?

MOTIA: The project is here also for the Forest Reserves, mind you. And when you talk about the reserves *[Beating his chest.]*, we are the custodians. Just as you are the custodians of the National Park.

Enter KONDO, carrying six bottles of beer.

KONDO: Era! *[...]* Koko! You surprise me a lot. Without any message? Not even my blood shook to warn me? *[To ASU and MOTIA.]* Gentlemen, meet my cousins.

ASU and MOTIA *[In unison, turning their faces away.]*: I see!

ERA: Look at him there. *[Mimicking, nasally.]* Gentlemen, meet my cousins. Foolish man.

KONDO: Is that how you've come, Era? Let me tell you, I won't put up with such behaviour any longer. *[Loudly.]* Not in my house. *[He sets down the beer bottles.]*

ERA *[Mimicking nasally.]*: Not in my house. Did you have a house before? Would you call what you had a house?

KOKO: He is the lucky type.

ERA: Lucky what? *[Pointing from ASU to MOTIA and to ASU again.]* These are the lucky ones. They have succeeded in grabbing all our benefits from the Korup Project. *[To KONDO.]* And you stay here giving them free beer everyday.

KONDO: There is more beer, if that is what you mean.

ERA: Beer? My father—I mean your uncle—is there troubling me with demands for this and that everyday. Was there a day that you remembered to send him even a rotten ten thousand francs to buy snuff?

KONDO: Is that not what we should be discussing privately, in a small family meeting?

ERA: Who has come to hold a meeting with you?

KONDO *[Angrily, stretching out his hands.]*: Please, give me your bags to keep in the house for you. My wife and children are still in the farm. And let me bring you chairs so you can sit down and share the drink with us.

ERA: Keep your chairs and drink to yourself.

KONDO: And you don't want to give me your bags?

ERA: We are crossing. *[With emphasis.]* To Mundemba Town. *[Surveys the house.]* Look at the type of house they have built for him. Is that what they described in the Master Plan?

KONDO: It is enough for me, Era.

ERA: If I were you I would have insisted that they built me something really nice. Like one of those beautiful houses in Mundemba Town. Of course, that's the deal.

KOKO: Was he not hurrying to get out?

KONDO: You continue to remain in there and wait for the best.

KOKO: What did you say?

ERA *[Already surveying the chairs.]*: I can see he is now living in such luxury. But tell those project friends of yours that they cannot lock a monkey and a bunch of ripe bananas in the same room and expect that monkey not to touch the bananas.

KONDO: What do you mean? Were you not also given the option to resettle? You caused the delay. And any thing could have happened that has eventually frustrate the plan.

ERA: Who even cares about resettlement again?

KOKO: We shall remain in there and continue to destroy.

ERA: Look, by the time they open their eyes to see what is happening, we will have wiped out everything [*Illustrating the point by wiping the mouth with his first finger and blowing air through at the same time.*].

KONDO [*In near whisper.*]: Have you already forgotten what happened to Koko and you the other day?

ERA casts KONDO an angry look, and then resumes surveying the house and chairs in hidden admiration. He is apparently boiling with regretful anger.

ERA [*Holds KOKO by the hand.*]: Let's get out of here.

KOKO: Why?

ERA: So you are interested in the drink, eh? Okay, you stay.

ERA starts walking away. KOKO follows.

KONDO: You even won't wait to see the family?

ERA [*Turns round.*]: We'll find another time and pay you a proper visit.

KONDO: My wife won't be happy to hear that you came around and could not even touch your buttocks on a chair.

ERA: What has she kept for us that is so special, Kondo? She can have everything. After all, is she not one of those people enjoying your money?

ERA and KOKO exit. MOTIA clicks his tongue in utter amazement.

MOTIA: Are they truly your cousins?

ASU: Still the same warriors!

MOTIA: They are simply jealous.

KONDO: Forget about them, gentlemen. Let's share our drink.

KONDO starts opening the beer. Meanwhile, ASU picks up the radio cassette and plays some music. Enter EKO and REKA.

MOTIA: Eko! Eko!

Everyone stands up and greets them. Discussion is in low tone, and is drowned by the sound of music. KONDO goes into the house and brings out two chairs. The music fades gradually into sustained softness.

ASU: These are your real cousins, Kondo. Not those....

KONDO: That's a family matter, Asu. *[To EKO and REKA.]* You're really lucky. You see I just opened the beer when you arrived.

MOTIA: It means that they've come with good hearts.

ASU: And it's a sign of good luck!

KONDO: Please, sit down and share with us.

Everyone else sits down while KONDO takes EKO's and REKA's bags into the house.

MOTIA: It's been such a long time.

EKO: Yes. Since the last big meeting.

ASU: Why have you decided to bury yourselves in there?

REKA: Is it that easy to come out?

EKO: You know all these things, Asu. You can't pretend that you don't. Dry season: farm work. Rainy season: flooded rivers. Often too flooded and too swift to cross. Not that easy to make pleasure trips, you know.

ASU: I know. Too bad. *[A short pause.]* So how's your committee getting on?

EKO: Slowly but steadily we're making some progress. Although there are some hunters who still cause us a lot of headache.

MOTIA: Such people can never be absent in any community.

ASU: Keep pushing on all the same. That's how we started. And with time….

Enter KONDO.

KONDO *[As he has resumed his seat, to EKO and REKA.]*: You've not had something to drink? *[...]* No one is drinking yet?

KONDO quickly opens drinks for EKO and REKA.

EKO *[Proposing a cheers, lifting up his beer.]*: For more blessings and more luck for Kondo.

Everyone lifts up their beer and does the traditional "cheers", each touching another's beer bottle with his.

KONDO *[After taking a sip, to EKO and REKA.]*: So tell me, what has brought you here?

EKO: What sort of question is that? Are we not supposed to pay you a visit and share in your joy?

REKA: Perhaps he's not happy to see us.

KONDO: No, Reka, no! *[In near whisper.]* On the contrary, I am so glad to receive you. Indeed, you have helped to renew my faith and confidence in that great family. *[A short pause.]* Cousins, if you met with Era and Koko and witnessed their behaviour towards me, you would know what I'm talking about. They refused to even sit down and share a drink with us. They left a while ago.

Silence.

EKO: Well, in any family you must expect people like

that. My only consolation is that you have at least benefited from the project before it has reached this stage when it is closing down.

ASU: What?

KONDO: I didn't quite get you, Eko.

EKO: So you have not heard the news? It started like a wild rumour, but now it has been confirmed.

REKA: My heart has become so heavy from the moment Eko gave me the news.

MOTIA [*Casually.*]: Where did you get the news?

EKO: Don't we have our own people working in the project? [*Silence.*] There was a big meeting to discuss the matter in Yaounde.

ASU: Are you saying that the Korup Project is closing down?

EKO: We-e-eh! How else do you want me to put it?

ASU [*Emotionally.*]: The Korup National Park and the three Forest Reserves, what will guarantee their protection? What is going to happen to our committee? What other source is there of its financial support?

EKO: Asu, you people are even lucky to have a committee that already has a solid foundation.

KONDO [*Shaking his head.*]: This is not possible! Ours is still a baby committee. What shall we do? Who will follow up our papers in Yaounde?

MOTIA: Let them go. Ever since they've been here, what have they really done in terms of development?

ASU: What are you saying, Motia?

MOTIA [*Stands up and takes a few steps.*]: Let them leave. Even now! Have you not consulted the Master Plan? Have they gone even half-way in terms of what they promised to do?

ASU: Like what? We have a road and a solid bridge. Have you ever made a trip to any other village around to see what the project has done? What else do you really want?

MOTIA: How do the schools and community halls benefit me?

ASU: I see. They should have built you a personal house, eh?

KONDO: Do you know I'm surprised to see you behave like this, Motia? Or are you already getting drunk? Look at my cousins here. They have received basically nothing from the project because....

MOTIA [*Starts walking away.*]: That's their own problem.

REKA: Is that what you can say?

EKO: Your heart is not clean, Motia.

MOTIA: You can say anything you wish. Whether the project is here or not, it doesn't really make any difference to me. *[He takes a few strides away.]*.

KONDO *[Ululating in amazement.]*: He is no different from my bad cousins.

MOTIA: I'm Nwana Mobeh. Far more dangerous than any of them. Though so calm. Take note. *[He exits.]*.

ASU: I am really ashamed! Motia, you make me very, very ashamed.

KONDO: Gentlemen, let's drink our beer and be happy.

ASU: Where can one find happiness at this point, my brother?

REKA: Right back in River Kotoro.

ASU: Exactly.

They continue drinking. Suddenly REKA stands up and intones a powerful traditional song and starts dancing. KONDO and EKO take up the chorus. ASU only joins in the handclapping. After a short while REKA kills the song in the traditional fashion, that is by suddenly stamping his right foot on the floor in front of the two and walking briskly back to his seat.

REKA *[As he is resuming his seat.]* We-e-eh! What can bring up the happiness again? What other source is there of hope?

[Pause.] When I heard about Korup and the resettlement programme, I thought my problems were over.

EKO: I still can't understand why the project is closing down?

ASU: What was actually discussed in that meeting?

REKA: And why was that sort of decision taken?

KONDO: I wonder!

Plangent sound of music.

Gradual Fadeout

Act Three

Scene Two [2003]

Yaounde. A big and well decorated conference room. Seated are MINISTER, PROJECT MANAGER, CONSERVATOR and DONOR representatives. Each meeting participant has a large nametag conspicuously displaced on the table in front of him. EU DONOR has just made a point.

PROJECT MANAGER: No. That is not true.

EU DONOR *[Firmly.]*: You can find that in black and white in the mid-term review report.

PROJECT MANAGER: Well, yes. But you should note that things have changed dramatically since that project review took place. We have been able to prepare management plans for the National Park and two of the Forest Reserves. *[Applause.]* In regard to the integrity of the National Park, Conservator is here to testify that we have continued to witness an enormous increase in wildlife sightings since last year. Due to reduced poaching. *[CONSERVATOR nods agreement.]*. We have also started receiving improved and increasing community support and participation. *[An applause.]* You see, we respond to community demands, providing development needs, such as….

EU DONOR: That is not acceptable! We are not here for that. You can't continue throwing things at people like that. We are not here to waste our money. We are not Father Christmas.

PROJECT MANAGER: You know it is very difficult to work with the local communities, using strict conservation parlance. You have to exploit other forms of dialogue, in order to win their support.

EU DONOR: That is not acceptable, I say. We are not here to bargain with the communities.

GTZ DONOR: I think we need to show some flexibility in dealing with the project.

EU DONOR [*Snapping back.*]: We have our long-standing set of policies and procedures. You either accept them or leave them.

PROJECT MANAGER: All the activities we carry out, sir, are part of our agreement with you. And I find it embarrassing for you to consider them as unapproved.

EU DONOR: I repeat, we are not Father Christmas.

Silence.

GTZ DONOR: I agree with you absolutely. We are not Father Christmas. But my fear is that if we continue to apply such rigid policies, the system that has taken so many years to build might collapse.

EU DONOR: Understand my point. And you should note that we have been here for too long. When is the Government going to take over at least some of the project activities? Can you not see that the Government has remained largely invisible and inactive in the Korup Project all this while?

MINISTER: I don't think so. The Government has Conservator to represent her in the project. And, as far as I know, there are many other Government staff seconded to the project. [To MANAGER.] Eh, Manager? [MANAGER, apparently angry with the whole thing, nods agreement.]

EU DONOR: Take note that these staff still continue to depend entirely on the project and donor funds to do their job, Mr. Minister.

PROJECT MANAGER: How else did you expect us to work together?

EU DONOR: The Government should provide funds for the National Park.

CONSERVATOR: The Government has a budget for the National Park, Mr. Donor. [EU DONOR turns his face away.] And I use this budget for the Park Service.

GTZ DONOR: Well, I think the government needs to put in some more.

EU DONOR: That is the point. At the moment, the Government is putting in very little or nothing. And the Park is for the benefit of the Government and its people.

MINISTER: Point of correction, sir. The Park is not only for the benefit of this country but also for the benefit of the whole world. And, gentlemen, let us not lose sight of the fact that the Government has yet to fully recover from her economic crisis. *[A short pause.]* And, besides, there are many priority areas where she puts in her best.

EU DONOR: By implication, Korup is not one of those priority areas, right?

MINISTER: Far from it. If Korup were not a priority area, there wouldn't be this steering committee meeting. *[A short pause.]* In fact, Korup is one of the top three conservation areas in our regional planning.

EU DONOR: But I don't see much of Government in Korup, to convince me.

PROJECT MANAGER: I know your argument is based on financial support. Otherwise, I should inform you that the Government seconded staff have proven to be very instrumental in the conservation and development efforts of the project.

GTZ DONOR: What has impressed me much is the creation of village-level natural resource management committees.

PROJECT MANAGER: That is an area I left out.

GTZ DONOR: It should be top priority, sir. Because these committees have the potential to save both the Korup National Park and the three Forest Reserves of Nta-Ali, Ejagham and Rumpi Hills.

PROJECT MANAGER: I agree with you totally. In fact, the committees have played a proactive role in combating poaching. They succeeded in evicting all foreign poachers, and are presently mounting pressure on indigenous poachers.

A thunderous applause.

GTZ DONOR: Keep up with the good work, Manager.

EU DONOR: I'm glad to hear about this new development. *[MANAGER and CONSERVATOR cast surreptitious glances at each other.]* But it's a pity that we've decided to be so stern at this encouraging moment in the history of Korup. The truth is I'm sick and tired of watching things go at a snail's pace.

MINISTER *[In a jocular manner.]*: I didn't know that some of you donors can be so stringent. *[EU DONOR gives a wry smile.]* Please, try to appreciate the difficulties in working with communities. *[GTZ DONOR nods in corroboration.]* From the reports you can see that some progress has been made.

EU DONOR: I agree with you totally. But my worry is that the Government is delaying the take-over of the project. For instance, our agreement was for the Government to take over the Park Guards that the project trained and hired, within the first five years of their engagement. But up until now, no one knows what the Minster is saying.

Phone ringing. Everyone touches their coat pockets to see if it is their mobile phones. MINISTER removes his mobile phone from his coat pocket and looks at it.

MINISTER *[Stands up.]*: Gentlemen, give me just a minute. I have an important call. *[He takes a few steps away and*

starts pacing up and down.] Hello! Hello! *[...]* Speaking. *[...]*
Monsieur le Ministre. *[Laughs.]* Maybe because of the battle
into which you've pushed me. *[...]* That's all right. *[...]* I know.
[...] Yes. *[...]* Ehn. *[...]* Ehn. *[...]* Never mind; it's part of the
job. *[...]* Well, I think some progress is being made. Only that,
as you know, the people are...Of course, you are even more
familiar with the type of atmosphere that prevails. *[...]* Yes.
Not really pleased with the Government. *[...]* Of course, you
should know better. Complaints about the minimal input and
commitment of Government. Especially this thing about
takeover. *[...]* Exactly. *[...]* Yes. *[…]* Ehn. So you know? *[...]*
And what are you doing about it? I think this is where the
problem lies *[...]* Yes. *[...]* Yes. *[…]* Are you sure? *[...]* Any
budget for that? *[...]* That's great news! I'll share it with
everyone here. This might tone down the temperature a little
bit. *[...]* All right. *[…]* That's right. *[…]* It's my pleasure. *[...]*
Have a nice day too. *[…]* Bye! *[Walks back to his seat smiling.]*
Hope I didn't take too much of your time, gentlemen.

ALL: Not at all.

MINISTER *[After resuming his seat.]*: Gentlemen, that was
the Minister of Environment and Forests. And I have
brought you a piece of news from him. *[A short pause.]* He is
taking over all the Park Guards in no time.

Another thunderous applause.

EU DONOR: That, at least, is a good sign. Arrangements
that guarantee the sustainability of the project activities have
been our yearning all these years.

GTZ DONOR: Absolutely. And this is an important first

step.

CONSERVATOR: The Park Adviser will be very glad to hear this. We've been struggling to reach this stage for years.

A pause.

MINISTER *[Jocularly, to EU DONOR.]*: I hope the Government has responded nicely this time.

EU DONOR: Yes. But I still have my doubts. It is not certain for how long we will have to wait yet again before it happens.

MINISTER: Oh, sorry! Sorry! I left out that. Actually, the Minister said the take-over will take effect in three months' time.

EU & GTZ DONORS *[In unison.]*: Unbelievable!

PROJECT MANAGER: I'm so surprised, indeed. It was such a battle for the project.

Enter YOUNG LADY carrying a tray containing biscuits, coffee and tea flasks, and tea cups. She sets them on a table in one corner of the room, and stands still, waiting to serve.

EU DONOR: This makes me a little more considerate. Because my intension was to stop my funding of the project completely. But as it stands, I think it's worthwhile continuing support for some of the project activities. *[A huge applause.]* But...*[Applause still.]* But *[Silence.]* this can only be done through the Government.

95

GTZ DONOR: Good idea. But I think we should consider a number of options and leave them open. For instance, we may want to continue our support through local NGOs.

EU DONOR: I totally agree with you.

GTZ DONOR: Gentlemen, let's give ourselves a big round of applause.

Applause.

MINISTER: Thank you very much, gentlemen. It's been such a productive session. I think everyone is a bit tired, and I can see the table ready for us. Can we, please, break off for coffee or tea.

Soft background music. Everyone rises and walks to the table. YOUNG LADY serves them with tea or coffee, as each pleases. They drink their tea or coffee as they stand or sit, discussing inaudibly in groups.

Gradual Fadeout
And End Of Play